# CREATING EMPLOYEE ENGAGEMENT

Self-coaching questions, inspiration, tips, and practical exercises for becoming an awesome manager

⌘

Managerial Competencies Series
Playbook No. 6

## CÉLESTE GRIMARD

Copyright © 2018 Céleste Grimard, Canada

All rights reserved. All materials on these pages are copyrighted by Céleste Grimard. Reproduction, modification, storage of all or part of this book in a retrieval system or retransmission, in any form or by any means, electronic, mechanical, or otherwise is strictly prohibited without prior written permission from the author. Although every effort has been made to indicate the sources of text and ideas, it's possible that we missed some! If you're aware of references or citations that haven't been provided, please contact the author. This book doesn't constitute legal advice and isn't a substitute for independent professional advice.

ISBN-13: 978-1979023467

## CreateSpace, Charleston, SC USA

# ⌘
# ACKNOWLEDGMENTS

I originally developed this series as a self-study, self-paced program for hundreds of managers working in a geographically dispersed area. Over the span of many years, these awesome managers offered me feedback, inspiration, and encouragement to transform this program into a series of practical, easy to read books accessible to all managers. Thank you! I also sincerely thank Rhiannon Ward for her assistance in editing and proofreading the books in this series.

# CONTENTS

Series Introduction 1

Introduction 3

1. Reality Check: Self-Coaching Questions 27

2. Inspiring Your Journey 39

3. Tips for Awesome Managers 45

4. Dilemmas: What Would You Do? 59

5. Planning For Action 67

About the Managerial Competencies Series 70

References 95

CREATING ENGAGEMENT

# Welcome to the Managerial Competencies Series!

The aim of this series is to help you understand and build the core competencies you need to become an awesome manager.

There's no getting around it. There are tons of journals, books, blogs, videos – you name it – on the topic of management. Yes, a lot has been written and said about how to be an effective manager. Everyone has their own spin to put on this topic, and research studies on this topic are practically endless. How does a busy manager sort through all the fads and fashions to find the nuggets of wisdom?

In designing this series, I pored over loads of resources and talked with hundreds of

# CREATING ENGAGEMENT

managers. I set aside all the fashions, fads, and fantasies, and I extracted only what is likely to be of enduring value to you. Although this series is geared towards practical, immediate use, I hope that it will provoke you to think deeply about managing and your role as a manager, and that it will make a difference for you so you can make a difference for others.

This module – Creating Engagement – is the sixth of 15 books, each covering a key competency of awesome managers. **Turn to page 70 to learn more about this series**, including the full slate of books, how each book is structured, and tips on how to get the most out of them.

Throughout the book, I will refer to your **learning journal** and your **feedback team. These helpful tools are explained on pages 85 and 86.**

# CREATING ENGAGEMENT: INTRODUCTION

Awesome managers help staff feel motivated to contribute their best to the organization.

# CREATING ENGAGEMENT

Why do some people work hard and others do as little as possible? What can you do to help your employees feel motivated to perform and engaged and committed?

Even in countries with better wages and working conditions than most, workers often suffer from low morale and productivity. This gap between an employee's actual and potential output has been called a "confidence gap" or a "commitment gap." Surveys have shown that, more often than not, employees want to do their best, but feel that "management" and "the system" prevent them from being successful. Often with the best of intentions, managers create the very conditions that result in poor morale, low productivity, and high frustration.

**Unpacking motivation** → Motivated people direct intense effort toward a particular goal in a persistent manner. So, motivation has three elements: the direction of behavior (what an

## CREATING ENGAGEMENT

employee is doing), intensity of action (how hard an employee is working), and persistence of effort over time (how long an employee works). We can't SEE *motivation*, rather we observe behaviors and the results of these behaviors, and that's what tells us whether someone is motivated or not.

**Contrary to popular belief, you can't motivate people to perform or behave in a certain way.** → There is no magic button or formula for getting people to do what you want them to do. People choose, either consciously or unconsciously to perform or behave. However, there are many things, both positive and negative, that you can do to influence these choices and create a motivational climate.

**Beware of motivational posters; they can be de-motivating!** → Theses posters entitled *Success* or *Teamwork* or some other theme and that present an inspirational message and an accompanying picture are meant to be

# CREATING ENGAGEMENT

motivational. However, if the posters contradict what is happening in a workplace, they serve as a source of de-motivation and cynicism. When accompanied by managerial practices that demonstrate that employees are truly valued, these posters aren't harmful, but they're not really needed either.

**Watch out for frustrated employees.** → They become unmotivated and disengaged employees. If all your employees were completely motivated to perform at their best, motivating them wouldn't be a problem. However, unless you're in a unique situation, you will have a motivational challenge with some or all of your employees at one time or another.

Most employees don't start out that way. Most want to work hard, be successful, contribute and accomplish things. They want to fill their needs through work, be secure, belong, win recognition, enjoy themselves, learn new skills, and work in a comfortable

# CREATING ENGAGEMENT

environment. Managers want the work to be done with as little fuss and cost as possible, and, sometimes, they pay attention to these end results more than the people who produce the results. Often what employees want from work is not what managers give them.

Do you or any of your employees:

→ Want to think for yourself rather than being told what to do?
→ Have ideas on how to organize and run things better?
→ Get bored with repetitive work?
→ Become unproductive when not challenged?
→ Become unhappy working at something when you don't see the results?
→ Come in late and leave early?
→ Hate being left out of important meetings?
→ Want someone to listen when you have suggestions or ideas?
→ Resent working with inadequate tools and equipment?
→ Want to have a say in how things turn out?

# CREATING ENGAGEMENT

→ Want to break off and have some fun?
→ Strive to learn new skills?
→ Want to be recognized for good work?

Frustration in any of these areas can produce de-motivated and discouraged employees.

**Consider why some employees perform poorly.**
→ Employees struggle to get the job done for one or more of the following reasons:

1. They don't know what to do or how to do it. Would their performance improve if they had more information, instruction or training?
2. Something or someone keeps them from it. Are there obstacles in your area, which, if removed or dealt with, would make it easier for these people to be successful?
3. They don't want to do it. Do you know why not? Is it dangerous, tedious, or uninteresting?

Think about your employees, and consider whether any of these reasons for poor performance fit. Aside from these reasons,

## CREATING ENGAGEMENT

there are some people who just can't perform. They may be emotionally or mentally unable to perform what is expected of them. Some may going through a temporary personal crisis that prevents them from contributing to their fullest. These employees require interventions other than what you as a manager can offer. An Employee Assistance Program may be an appropriate place to start.

**Be careful what you expect, you may get it!** → How you manage people tells us a lot about your beliefs about the basic nature of people. If you believe that people are lazy and basically hate to work, then you'll watch over your employees like a hawk. As a result, employees will feel little responsibility for their work and may only work hard when you're around. It's comparable to the set-up-to-fail syndrome illustrated on the next page and described by management researchers Jean-François Manzoni and Jean-Louis Barsoux in their *Harvard Business Review* article.

# CREATING ENGAGEMENT

## The Set-Up-To-Fail Syndrome
A Negative Self-Fulfilling Prophecy in Action

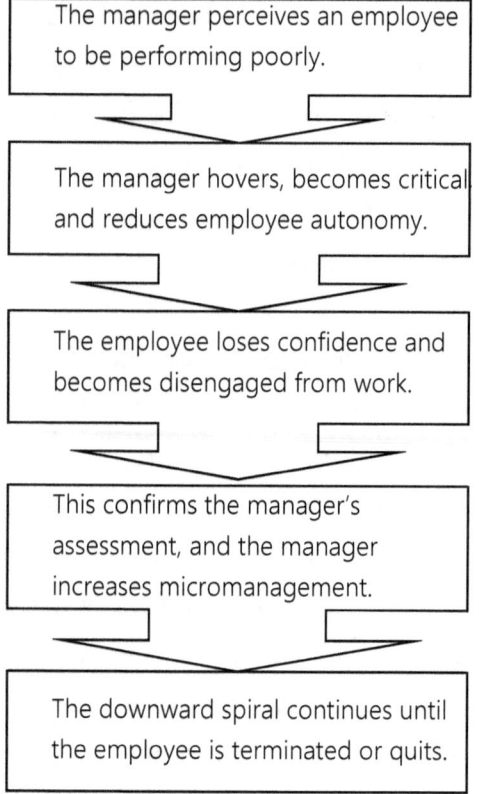

(From "The Set-Up-To-Fail Syndrome" by Manzoni & Barsoux, published in *Harvard Business Review*.)

## CREATING ENGAGEMENT

**Build a positive self-fulfilling prophecy.** → On the other hand, if you assume that people want meaningful, fulfilling, and responsible work, this will be reflected in the kind of work that you give them. If you think your employees want challenging work, then you're more likely to give them the feedback, resources, and support needed for them to accomplish challenging tasks. They, in turn, will consider your actions to be a vote of confidence for them and will develop a sense of self-efficacy or confidence. This will help them accomplish the tasks that, in turn, fulfill your expectations.

**Think about your core beliefs about people.** → Are you a Theory X or a Theory Y person? In his classic research, Douglas McGregor developed these theories as a way of helping managers examine their personal beliefs about the nature of the people.

Theory X assumptions cause managers to conceive of their role in terms of two

## CREATING ENGAGEMENT

extremes: hard and soft management, both of which McGregor views as irrelevant. Hard management is characterized by the use of tight controls and close supervision. It produces restricted work output, antagonism, and subtle undermining of organizational objectives. Soft management is demonstrated by managers who consider their role to be satisfying people's demands, being extremely permissive, and maintaining harmony. It results in managers abdicating their responsibilities and generating ineffective employees.

Under Theory Y, the emphasis is on self-control or internally controlled employees. Theory Y implies that, within a climate of trust and respect, employees are capable of putting forth willing effort and controlling their work habits. This suggests that workers' needs (such as meaningful work, personal freedom, esteem and creative expression) are best met by directing their energies toward organizational goals.

# CREATING ENGAGEMENT

| Theory X | Theory Y |
|---|---|
| \multicolumn{2}{c}{Most people...} | |

| Theory X | Theory Y |
|---|---|
| Dislike work and want as little to do as possible | Want meaningful work |
| Are lazy and unambitious | Like responsibility |
| Dislike responsibility | Will adapt to change |
| Resist change | Are primarily motivated by challenging work |
| Are primarily motivated by money | Prefer self-direction |
| Prefer to be directed | Are creative |
| Have little creativity | |

A manager should...

| Theory X | Theory Y |
|---|---|
| Plan, organize, direct and closely control the efforts of people | Involve employees in planning, organizing and controlling their own efforts |
| Make most of the important decisions | Delegate the authority needed to make decisions |
| Punish mistakes | Focus on resolving problems, not punishing mistakes |
| Not get too close to employees | |
| Assume that their authority is unquestionable | Know each employee personally |

# CREATING ENGAGEMENT

**Help employees satisfy their three basic needs.**
→ People tend to be motivated to fulfill unsatisfied needs. Beyond basic survival needs, there are three types of needs: affiliation, achievement, and power. In developing his popular needs theory, psychologist David McClelland argued that, although people are motivated by all of these needs, people differ in how important each of the needs are to them. For example, although achievement may be an employee's strongest need, affiliation or power may be more important to another employee. This means that managers need to figure out which needs are especially important to an employee and then find ways to satisfy those needs.

# CREATING ENGAGEMENT

**People with a high need for achievement...**

Want challenging but doable tasks.

Want a reasonable degree of control over results (so, they dislike situations where chance plays a big role and where performance strongly depends on others).

Want opportunities for self-direction.

Want frequent feedback regarding their performance (preferably from the task itself rather than from others).

Want to be able to plan their work, see projects to their completion, and meet deadlines.

Tend to persevere and are motivated primarily by task accomplishment rather than financial gain.

**People with a high need for affiliation...**

Tend to be friendly and outgoing.

Are motivated by the opportunity to develop and maintain harmonious interpersonal relationships.

Seek out others (unlike achievers who aren't as keen to work in groups and don't mind working alone).

Are especially attentive to the impact of decisions on people and their interrelationships.

**People with a high need for power...**

Like to take charge of situations and be in control.

Set directions (via goals) and enjoy influencing others through argument or by other means in the pursuit of these goals.

Tend to adopt more autocratic decisions and a win/lose approach to handling differences of opinion.

# CREATING ENGAGEMENT

What about you? What is your highest need? What is your lowest need?

> **A Quick Test of Your Need for Achievement**
>
> Imagine that you're playing a Ring Toss game. You're tossing rings over a peg from any distance you choose. What distance would you choose?
> a. Close to the peg.
> b. Far away from the peg.
> c. A moderate distance from the peg.
>
> The answer is on page 20.

**A need for achievement is central to ... achievement.** → McClelland considered achievement to be central to individual success and even national economic performance. His research found a strong relationship between a high need for achievement and high performance levels. This means that it's

## CREATING ENGAGEMENT

important to boost your employees' need for achievement (and your own).

**But, be sensitive to cultural differences in the need to achieve.** → The importance of the need to achieve may be culture bound. Although western cultures tend to stress the importance of *doing*, many other cultures value *being*. In such cultures, the aim is not to work hard to achieve outcomes; rather it is to work enough to enjoy life as it is happening. They work to live, rather than live to work.

| **Doing** *versus* | **Being** |
|---|---|
| Control | Flow |
| Plan and organize | Live for the moment |
| Achieve the most in life | Experience life |
| Short-term planning | Long-term planning |
| Maximize work | Minimize work |

Source: Nancy Adler, *International dimensions of organizational behavior.*

# CREATING ENGAGEMENT

**Remember that all people have a need for belonging.** → Although McClelland directed his attention to the need for achievement, other researchers found that the need for affiliation was the most fundamental and pervasive motivator of all. In their extensive review of existing research, social psychologists Roy Baumeister and Mark Leary found that people need "frequent, nonaversive interactions within an ongoing relational bond." Their research also strongly linked a sense of belonging with physical, emotional, and psychological well-being. A poor sense of belonging was associated with a wide range of adjustment and health difficulties.

**Who makes the best managers?** → A high need for achievement is associated with effectiveness for lower level managers whose accomplishments may be more dependent on their personal performance than on their ability to persuade others to perform. Managers with high affiliation needs combined with low

## CREATING ENGAGEMENT

power needs tend to have low performing work units. Apparently, their need for approval and to be liked by others strongly influences their decisions. As a result, these managers come across as being inconsistent and unfair. A certain level of the need for power is required to be a manager. However, those with a need for "socialized" power tend to be more effective than those with a need for "personal" power.

Managers with a socialized need for power are altruistic: they want to use power for the good of others and the organization, not for their own glorification. Their satisfaction comes from helping others achieve goals rather than from their own personal successes. Those with a personal need for power aren't effective managers because they tend to be domineering, manipulative, self-serving, and excessively concerned with getting credit for successes.

In sum, effective managers have a particular pattern of needs: a high socialized

# CREATING ENGAGEMENT

need for power and a low to moderate need for affiliation and personal achievement.

> **Here's the answer to "A Quick Test of Your Need for Achievement":** People with a high need for achievement set moderately challenging goals for themselves (answer C). They would not choose a throwing distance that makes the task too easy or impossible.

**What you reward gets done!** → As management researcher, Steven Kerr wrote in his seminal article, "On the folly of rewarding A, while hoping for B," sometimes we reward the opposite of what we want. We hope for teamwork, innovation, creativity, and honesty, but we reward conformity and individual accomplishments as well as maintenance of the status quo without errors. We hope employees will demonstrate people skills, but we reward technical accomplishments. We hope for employee involvement, but we maintain control over operations.

## CREATING ENGAGEMENT

**Ensure that your employees' efforts lead to effective performance, and they receive adequate and desirable rewards for their performance.** → According to Vroom's Expectancy Theory, people choose their behavior based on their perceptions of the likelihood that a particular behavior will bring them valued outcomes. In other words, people make choices about the level at which they perform. They do so based on the amount of effort that provides them with the best possible outcomes. People do what gets rewarded and avoid things that aren't rewarded or that are punished. There are three important linkages:

① Effort → Performance Expectations, the extent to which effort results in task performance levels.

② Performance → Outcome Instrumentality, a belief that performance results in consequences such as rewards or punishments.

③ Valence, how much a person values an outcome. People value outcomes

# CREATING ENGAGEMENT

differently due to differences in strengths for particular needs.

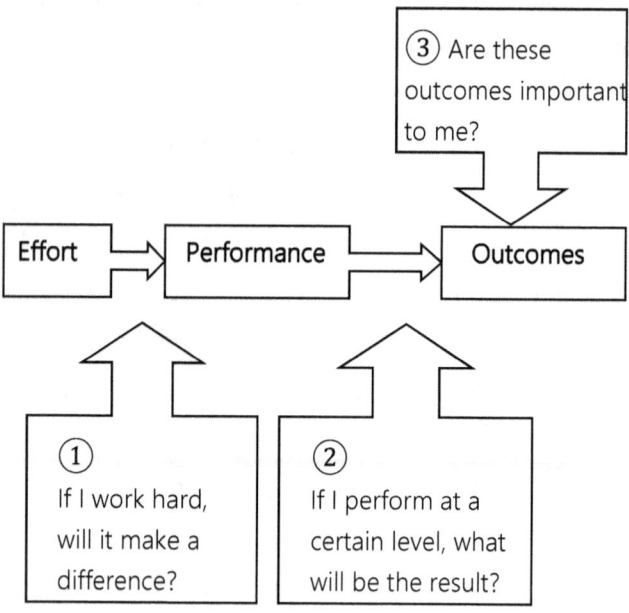

Managers must ensure that all three linkages exist since all are needed for employees to perform at high levels. If one or more linkage is missing, lower levels of motivation occur. For example, if people perform but don't receive desired outcomes or are even punished, this reduces their future motivation.

## CREATING ENGAGEMENT

**Help your employees work towards well-defined goals.** → Goals are specific results or outcomes that are anticipated. Goals that lead to high performance are:
1. Specific (explicit and measurable; e.g., reduce turnover levels to 5% NOT do your best);
2. Challenging but doable (realistic, given available resources);
3. Bound by time limits to provide a sense of urgency (e.g., complete this project by November 1$^{st}$ NOT complete this project in the near future);
4. Established in a participative manner rather than imposed or assigned; this provides employees with a better understanding and increased commitment to the goals;
5. Accompanied by feedback that is immediate, frequent, and, ideally, generated by the tasks themselves (rather than from external sources).

According to Locke and Latham's Goal Setting Theory, goals help employees know where to

## CREATING ENGAGEMENT

direct their attention, and they stimulate effort and encourage task persistence.

**Give employees meaningful work to do.** →
Meaningful work involves:
1. Performing a variety of tasks, each requiring its own skill set; for example, designing menus, addressing specialized dietary needs, and managing the dietary unit instead of just doing one of these tasks. (Skill variety)
2. Completing a whole piece of work; for example, being responsible for all aspects of a project from start to finish instead of only one step of the project. (Task identity)
3. Doing work that has significance; for example, work that has an impact on the lives of others. (Task significance)

Variety, task identity, and task significance help employees feel that their work is meaningful and worthwhile.

## CREATING ENGAGEMENT

**Help employees feel a sense of personal responsibility for the outcomes of their work by giving them some autonomy in carrying it out.** → Autonomy is the extent to which a job is performed without a great deal of supervision and intervention from others; for example, being allowed to schedule client appointments and determine how to carry out those appointments instead of simply following well-defined procedures regarding how to schedule and carry out appointments.

**Help employees know the results of their work activities.** → Feedback lets employees know, on a regular basis, that they are doing a good job. Ideally, performance feedback is provided by the job itself.

**For optimal motivation, combine all 5 of these characteristics (variety, task identity, task significance, autonomy, and feedback).** → According to Hackman and Oldham's Job Characteristics Model, all of these result in a

## CREATING ENGAGEMENT

sense of motivation, high levels of job performance and satisfaction, and lowered absenteeism and turnover. All five of these characteristics must be present in order for motivation to occur; in other words, high levels in one or more of the characteristics don't compensate for low levels in any one of them.

CREATING ENGAGEMENT

# 1

# REALITY CHECK: SELF-COACHING QUESTIONS

To help you examine your motivational skills and challenges, we invite you to ask yourself a series of self-coaching questions. While thinking about your behavior in the past six months, find specific examples that support your answers. Consider whether or not

## CREATING ENGAGEMENT

"counter examples" exist; in other words, times when you may not have behaved in a manner that is consistent with your answer. In answering these questions, think about how you generally are rather than temporary aberrations due to stress or other factors.

Your answers to these self-coaching questions will shine a light on how you see yourself. If you know yourself well, your answers will be right on the mark. However, many people don't have accurate self-perceptions because they're not used to assessing themselves, they feel uncomfortable with the idea of reflecting on their own behaviors, or they truly don't know themselves well. As a result, their answers may be *extremely* inflated or low.

In all cases, but especially when answers are extreme (in any direction), seeking candid and honest feedback from others can be a valuable way of shedding light on your actual competency levels. You can learn a lot more about yourself if you get feedback from others.

## CREATING ENGAGEMENT

You can ask people to answer some of the self-coaching questions for you and provide examples or anecdotes of situations that illustrate their answers. They may not tell you what you want to hear, but it may be exactly what you need to help you make progress on your journey toward becoming an awesome manager. As American writer Herbert Sebastian Aga said in his book *A Time for Greatness*, "the truth that makes men free is, for the most part, the truth which men prefer not to hear."

Asking others for feedback takes courage on everyone's part. Others don't necessarily have the same picture of you as you have of yourself, and people are sometimes reluctant to "tell it like it is." However, "feedback-lite" that is polite and tells you what you hope to hear won't help you grow as a person. Tell people that you need the straight goods (politely though!).

CREATING ENGAGEMENT

# Motivating Conditions

- → Do I greet each person pleasantly every day?
- → When I talk to people, do I make eye contact and speak respectfully and pleasantly?
- → Do I ask for others' advice on matters concerning their job, work area, or other related items?
- → Do I treat everyone equally? Or, do I play favorites?
- → Do I share information with all team members? Or, do I withhold information from any team member?
- → Do I assign a reasonable workload to all? Or, do I tend to assign an overload of work without including essential people in the decision-making process?
- → Do I praise people publicly who have done good work?
- → Do I correct people privately on mistakes

## CREATING ENGAGEMENT

or a job done poorly?
→ Do I offer coaching to improve job performance and teach new skills?
→ Do I insist on high standards and communicate that respectfully?
→ Am I an efficient manager?
→ Do I encourage and teach my staff to think for themselves?
→ Do I arrange work tasks so that staff can see the end results of their efforts?
→ Do I divide work tasks to make them as interesting as possible?
→ Do I listen when there are ideas on how to do things better?
→ Do I inform people about what is going on in the organization?
→ Do I treat my people as professionals in their areas at all times?
→ Do I recognize my staff for good work, both formally and informally?
→ Do I offer challenges whenever possible?
→ Do I encourage and provide opportunities for personal and skill development?

## CREATING ENGAGEMENT

Now, still thinking about the last six months, **re-visit the previous questions and answer them while thinking about how your boss treats you**. For example, does your boss greet you pleasantly each day? Does your boss recognize good work, both formally and informally?

These questions, when applied first to you as a manager and then to your boss, evaluate whether you see yourself and your boss as creating motivating working conditions. If you agreed with many or all of the questions, this is the ideal situation! You feel engaged and motivated at work, and you probably pass it on to your employees. But, if your working conditions are de-motivating, you're likely to continue that pattern with your employees. Unless you act as a buffer and resist passing on any negative treatment to your employees, they are likely to suffer – indirectly – from de-motivating working conditions as well.

CREATING ENGAGEMENT

# Assumptions about People

While thinking about people in general, consider how much you agree with the following statements.

→ Even when given encouragement by the boss, few people show a desire to improve themselves on the job.
→ If you give people enough money, they are less likely to worry about intangibles such as status or recognition.
→ Because most people don't like to make decisions on their own, it's hard to get them to assume responsibility.
→ Being tough with people will usually get them to do what you want.
→ It's too much to expect that people will try to do a good job without being prodded and closely supervised by their boss.
→ Bosses who expect their people to set their own standards for superior performance

## CREATING ENGAGEMENT

will probably find that they don't set them very high.
→ One problem in asking for employees' ideas is that their perspective is too limited for their suggestions to be of much practical value.
→ It is only human nature for people to try to do as little work as they can get away with.

This series of questions examines your assumptions about people, their work, and how to get people to work. If you agreed with most of the statements, you lean toward an autocratic management style and Theory X assumptions about people. You believe that people take little initiative on their own and must be watched carefully and closely controlled.

If you mostly disagreed with the statements, you favor Theory Y assumptions about people, and you tend toward a more developmental managerial style. You assume that people enjoy their work and are eager to accept responsibility and monitor their own performance.

A management style on either extreme, either too controlling or too permissive, will probably not be effective. Although most employees, fundamentally, want challenging responsibilities, over time, some may have developed a work style where they simply respond to orders rather than taking initiative. In the latter case, you may need to work towards adopting a developmental style in a gradual manner.

# Work Needs

The following questions were adapted from a longer self-assessment found in the *Structured Experiences Kit*. For each question, choose the option (a, b, or c) that best describes how you generally are.

# CREATING ENGAGEMENT

1. When solving a problem, do I like to:
   a. work by myself and be solely responsible for the solution?
   b. work as part of a team and find a team solution?
   c. work as part of a team, but only if I'm in charge?

2. In discussions, I like to:
   a. focus on problem-solving.
   b. get to know my fellow workers better.
   c. take an opposing view just as a matter of interest.

3. I like getting feedback that:
   a. is specific about how well I have done a job.
   b. is about how well I've worked with others as a team.
   c. takes the form of raises or promotions; I'm the best judge of how well I have done a job.

## CREATING ENGAGEMENT

4. Pick a quote:
    a. "Nothing succeeds like success."
    b. "Do not step on people on the way up; you may meet them on the way down."
    c. "Nobody remembers the name of the person who came in second in a race."

5. I work best:
    a. when I have deadlines to meet.
    b. when I have a personal relationship with my manager.
    c. in situations in which I am my own boss.

These questions assess your needs, according to McClelland's Needs Theory. If you responded with mostly As, your top need is Achievement. Mostly Bs indicates a hig need for Affiliation. Mostly Cs means your need for Power is highest. For more information, review the text related to this needs theory.

CREATING ENGAGEMENT

# Reality Check Reflection

1. What do your answers indicate about how you prefer to "motivate" others?
2. What have others said about your skills in this area?
3. To what extent do your personal views and those of others overlap?

CREATING ENGAGEMENT

# 2

# INSPIRING YOUR JOURNEY

As you read through the following quotations, take note of the ones that speak to you the most. Then consider the message they are conveying to you.

## CREATING ENGAGEMENT

In order to willingly accept the direction of another individual, it must feel good to do so. This business of making another person feel good in the unspectacular course of his daily comings and goings is, in my view, the very essence of leadership. - *John Frederman*

⌘

Make everyone a hero. Remembering to recognize, reward, and celebrate accomplishments is a critical leadership skill. And it is probably the most underutilized motivational tool in organizations. There is no limit to how much recognition you can provide, and it is often free.
- *Rosabeth Moss Kanter*

⌘

If we did all the things we were capable of doing, we would literally astound ourselves.
- *Thomas Edison*

⌘

You cannot raise a man up by calling him down. - *William Boetcker*

## CREATING ENGAGEMENT

Motivation is like food for the brain. You cannot get enough in one sitting. It needs continual and regular top ups. - *Peter Davies*

⌘

Trivial rewards will result in trivial amounts of effort. - *David Nadler and Edward Lawler, III*

⌘

We are most likely to become enthusiastic about what we are doing when we are free to decide how we do it. - *A. Cohen*

⌘

You've got to think about big things while you're doing small things so that all the small things go in the right direction. - *Alvin Toffler*

⌘

What you get by achieving your goals is not as important as what you become by achieving your goals. - *Henry David Thoreau*

⌘

The only way to do great work is to love what you do. - *Steve Jobs*

## CREATING ENGAGEMENT

Community in the workplace is nurtured whenever we enable people to feel connected ... Our goal is to generate in people a sense of belonging and loyalty ... As manager-leaders recognize mutual connectedness and build community within the organization, they will sow the seeds for extending that sense of belonging to the larger communities to which the organization belongs.
- *Carole Napolitano & Lida Henderson*

⌘

People often say that motivation doesn't last. Well, neither does bathing. That's why we recommend it daily. - *Zig Ziglar*

⌘

Few things can help an individual more than to place responsibility on him and to let him know that you trust him.
- *Booker T. Washington*

⌘

It always seems impossible until it's done.
- Nelson Mandela

## CREATING ENGAGEMENT

### Donkey in the Well

One day a farmer's donkey fell into a well. The animal cried piteously for hours as the farmer tried to figure out what to do. Finally he decided the animal was old, and the well needed to be covered up anyway. All his neighbors came over, grabbed a shovel, and began to shovel dirt into the well. At first, the donkey realized what was happening and cried horribly. Then, to everyone's amazement, he quieted down. A few shovel loads later, the farmer looked down the well and was astonished at what he saw. With every shovel of dirt that hit his back, the donkey would shake it off and take a step up. Soon, the donkey stepped up over the edge of the well and trotted off!

Life is going to shovel dirt on you, all kinds of dirt. The trick to getting out of the well is to shake it off and take a step up. Each of our troubles is a stepping-stone. We can get out of the deepest wells just by not stopping, never giving up. - *Author Unknown*

## CREATING ENGAGEMENT

What are your five favorite quotations?

Why do these stand out for you?

Which would you want to adopt as your personal motto? Include on the signature line of your emails? Post on your desk?

CREATING ENGAGEMENT

# 3

# TIPS FOR AWESOME MANAGERS

As you review the following tips for creating engagement, circle, check or highlight those that are especially meaningful for you.

## CREATING ENGAGEMENT

1. Begin with motivating yourself. It's hard to create motivational working conditions for others when you're feeling apathetic and uninterested in your own work. You need to serve as a good example for your employees.

**Interpersonal Climate**

2. Create a friendly and welcoming working environment. Pay attention to how your employees socialize and work together, and address any conflicts, cliques, socially isolated individuals, or other interpersonal issues that may be developing.

3. Provide regular opportunities for your employees to get together to engage in team problem-solving and decision-making.

4. Hold gatherings, get-togethers, and other occasions for social interaction.

## CREATING ENGAGEMENT

5. Back up and support your employees when representing them to others. Be loyal to your employees.

6. Talk up your employees to others. This is a way of showing pride in them and supporting them. Let others know about your employees' accomplishments. Contribute articles on your employees' accomplishments to the organizational newsletter.

7. Be understanding when your employees make well-intentioned mistakes. Support employees during times of stress.

8. Take an interest in employees beyond their work, but don't pry or interfere in their private lives.

9. Care about your employees as individuals. Don't expect employees to commit to the organization at the expense of their family

## CREATING ENGAGEMENT

obligations. Don't expect them to spend most of their waking time at work.

10. Be attentive to employees' needs and motivations. Understand individual differences in what motivates them (ask and listen).

11. Show your employees that they matter (i.e. that they are important and wanted).

12. Be interested in what your employees are doing. Be approachable, not distant.

13. Treat your employees as though they are central to the success of your organization (they are!) Employees can only treat clients as well as they have been treated themselves.

14. Hold team-building and other sessions that help your employees work more effectively as a team.

## CREATING ENGAGEMENT

**Involvement**

15. Listen to employees and try to understand the work situation from their perspectives.

16. Ask for and be open to feedback and suggestions. Invite employees to participate in decisions that affect them.

17. Involve employees in setting goals (identifying what performance means) and suggesting ways to get their work done.

18. When making unpopular decisions, explain your rationale to your employees, and listen to what they have to say.

19. Help employees see the bigger picture of how they are making a difference in people's lives and contributing to organizational objectives.

## CREATING ENGAGEMENT

20. Provide information about what is happening in the organization, how well the organization is doing, industry developments, new procedures, etc.

21. Encourage your employees to participate in industry trade shows and events.

**Work Performance**

22. Determine what level of performance you want; that is, what good performance means to you in specific terms. Develop good measures of performance. Clearly identify expected behaviors and results. Ensure that your expectations are challenging but attainable.

23. Describe specific outcomes that employees can expect as a result of their performance. Explicitly link performance to outcomes ("If you do this, you get this").

## CREATING ENGAGEMENT

24. Ensure that employees have the resources needed to succeed – personal (skills, knowledge), support, and material (equipment, funding, etc.).

25. Ensure that employees have the skills needed to perform at the expected level. Provide any needed training.

26. Ensure that there aren't any policies, procedures, or other issues that prevent employees from doing their work effectively. Ask employees what is preventing them from achieving their performance goals, and address these issues.

27. Ensure that employees don't feel pressure (from other employees or other sources) to maintain a level of performance that is below their capacity.

# CREATING ENGAGEMENT

28. Provide employees with access to resources, information, and any support necessary to carry out a task.

29. Provide employees with the ability to obtain others' cooperation in doing their work (authority, support, etc.).

30. Provide employees with discretion and visibility.

31. Observe and measure performance levels. Ask employees to keep track of their performance levels and accomplishments.

32. When you need to address issues of poor performance, do so in a professional manner:
    a. Treat employees with respect.
    b. Make reprimands in private, not in public.
    c. Address specific behaviors rather than assassinating the person's character.

## CREATING ENGAGEMENT

   d.  Provide coaching when needed.

33. Where possible, combine tasks to increase skill variety and task identity.

34. Allow employees to engage in job rotation so that they can build their skill sets and a broader appreciation of how the organization functions.

35. Acknowledge parts of employees' jobs that aren't intrinsically motivating. Some aspects of jobs are naturally less interesting than others. Granting that this is the case shows employees that you appreciate their efforts.

36. Provide some choice, where possible, as to how your employees do their work.

## CREATING ENGAGEMENT

**Recognition and Feedback**

37. Provide feedback on how employees are doing immediately after the desired behavior has been demonstrated. Ensure that it is specific and constructive.

38. Find out what rewards employees value. This can be determined by directly asking employees or by observing employees' reactions in different situations.

39. Provide rewards as promised but only for desired performance.

40. Ensure that your motivational approach is fair. Preferential treatment should not be given to your favorite employees. Good performers should get more rewards than poor performers.

41. Take your employees out to lunch or host a pot-luck lunch in the staff lunch room.

## CREATING ENGAGEMENT

42. Express appreciation on a regular basis. Don't wait for instances of extraordinary accomplishment.

43. Be appreciative of those whose work isn't in the spotlight (for example, support staff).

44. Celebrate accomplishments and "small victories." Find reasons to have informal recognition celebrations with light refreshments.

45. Send handwritten thank-you notes in recognition of special effort.

46. Have a special recognition bulletin board for thank-you cards, letters from customers, and other indicators of contribution.

# CREATING ENGAGEMENT

## De-Motivating Behaviors

47. Avoid the following interpersonal mistakes:
    a. Giving perks and other preferential treatment to a few employees.
    b. Intimidating, belittling, or humiliating employees.
    c. Yelling or swearing at employees, or having angry outbursts or tantrums.
    d. Throwing items at employees, or pushing and grabbing them.
    e. Threatening employees verbally and/or non-verbally.
    f. Using sarcasm or teasing.
    g. Talking down to employees.
    h. Persistently interrupting employees, or preventing them from expressing themselves.
    i. Giving employees the silent treatment.

## CREATING ENGAGEMENT

48. Avoid the following undermining behaviors:
    a. Ordering employees to stay late.
    b. Taking credit for employees' successes.
    c. Inappropriately accusing employees of wrongdoing.
    d. Making jokes at the expense of employees.
    e. Revealing employees' private information to others.
    f. Spreading rumors about employees.
    g. Blaming employees for others' errors.
    h. Showing little interest in employees and their opinions.
    i. Ignoring or excluding employees and their contributions.

# CREATING ENGAGEMENT

49. Don't make it difficult for employees to do their work:
    a. Not returning phone calls or responding to memos in a reasonable period of time.
    b. Withholding necessary information.
    c. Setting impossible deadlines.
    d. Shifting goals without informing employees beforehand.
    e. Undervaluing employees' efforts.
    f. Removing employees' areas of responsibility without consultation.

CREATING ENGAGEMENT

# 4

# DILEMMAS: WHAT WOULD YOU DO?

This section gives you the opportunity to apply what you've just learned. Read all of the following situations, and then answer the reflection questions in your learning journal. Then, explain why you answered the way you did and how you might apply this at work.

# CREATING ENGAGEMENT

## The Despondent Lab Technician

Paulette isn't looking forward to another day at work. She thought about calling in sick, but realized that this would only cause problems for herself and others. Her job as a lab technician has become fairly routine for her. Although the names on the specimen sample containers differs from day to day, the types of analyses that she performs are always the same – blood test here; urinalysis there. She feels that she could do her job with her eyes closed – but she doesn't. She is very attentive to details and concerned about the impact of making a mistake.

When she first started her job five years ago, Paulette felt challenged by her work. Every day presented her with new learning experiences. At the end of the day, she would cheerfully reflect on the volume and quality of work she had done, and she would feel a sense of pride in her accomplishments. Eventually, however, the work became mundane. Paulette

## CREATING ENGAGEMENT

began feeling impatient with the ever-increasing and never-ending workload, resentful towards doctors who insisted on having their analyses performed before others that were in the queue, and bitter about having been passed up for a promotion in favor of the lab manager's friend.

A year ago, Paulette agreed to be a member of an organization-wide team that considered how to boost staff morale. She was instrumental in introducing a "Commitment to Excellence" program that involved brief in-service seminars on teamwork, service quality, and leadership; posters and other materials that promoted the excellence theme; and an Excellence in Action award. Employees were encouraged to "catch someone doing something right" and then nominate these co-workers for an award. Every Thursday morning, the CEO of the Health Center and Paulette would make a surprise visit to a work unit and present an employee with a certificate and a health center pin. The recipients were always

# CREATING ENGAGEMENT

thrilled to receive the award and the CEO's attention. For her part, Paulette enjoyed seeing the glow on their faces and spending some time with the CEO. Although the program began with a flurry of activity, after six months, there were no more nominations. "Is no one doing anything right?" Paulette wondered. She had overheard that a couple people had received nominations from their best friends and that one other recipient had done "only one thing right" in the 10 years that he had been there.

**The Cynical Intake Clerk**

Raymond, an intake clerk in the emergency ward of the Health Center, complains that the Commitment to Excellence program means nothing to him – it doesn't give him more money, reduce his workload, or help him deal with impatient patients or his micromanaging supervisor. Apparently, his supervisor had heard about "managing by walking around" at

## CREATING ENGAGEMENT

a workshop, but interpreted this to mean that she needed to ask Raymond how things were going on an hourly basis and generally hover over Raymond's work area. Although Raymond sometimes wishes that his supervisor would "manage by walking away," at the same time, he really isn't sure what she expects from him. When he asks her if there is a particular length of time that it should take to "process a patient" or if there were any other standards that he should be meeting, she just tells him to do his best, and she walks away. It doesn't seem to matter if he works slowly or quickly. He gets his annual increment in salary, nothing more and nothing less.

However, he knows that he has to work "happily" – or, at least, appear to be happy. Once when his supervisor asked him how he was doing, he replied, "Good." She became quite adamant that he say that everything was "absolutely wonderful." She wanted to be seen as the successful supervisor of a happy team in a happy workplace and, eventually, become

# CREATING ENGAGEMENT

the CEO of a happy health center.

After Raymond had been in his job for only a month, he became aware of the existence of a clique in his work unit. The members of this group had all started in the work unit at about the same time. They socialized with each other after work and formed a "voting block" at team meetings. Although their objective performance levels were probably below that of Raymond and his coworkers, they always actively supported the supervisor in everything she said and did and, thus, were provided with special "incentives" such as preferred shift schedules and access to training. Prior to this work experience, Raymond had considered himself to be a people person and had easily developed friendships with his coworkers and warm relationships with his supervisors. He couldn't understand what he was doing wrong.

CREATING ENGAGEMENT

## The Invisible Cleaning Person

Gilles doesn't have much to say about the Commitment to Excellence program. He just wants to do his job. He spends his days mopping up floors, picking up garbage, and washing various surfaces. He follows a strict routine every day and takes comfort in its unchanging nature. He appreciates that he has had steady work at the Health Center for the past 25 years that allows him to raise his family at a reasonable standard of living.

His day-to-day work existence is quiet. He generally goes about doing his work without any interaction with anyone. He prefers to not draw any attention to himself, and he makes himself as invisible as possible. When a doctor throws something on the floor, he picks it up, grateful to have work to do. He would say, "That's what I'm here for. Those doctors have important things to do."

# CREATING ENGAGEMENT

Every once in a while, a patient or doctor would greet or say thank you to Gilles, and this would make his day. His primary satisfactions in life come from being with his family and being a member of a men's organization sponsored by his church. Although not an outgoing person, Gilles enjoys being around people, and people appreciate his easygoing manner.

**Reflection Questions**

1. How would you describe Paulette, Raymond, and Gilles' situations using the ideas presented in this book?
2. If you were Paulette, Raymond, or Gilles' supervisor, what top three actions would you take to establish motivational working conditions? Explain how these actions would be beneficial.
3. How could these actions and strategies apply to your staff and workplace?

CREATING ENGAGEMENT

# 5

# PLANNING FOR ACTION

Write your answers to the following questions in your learning journal.

# CREATING ENGAGEMENT

## Part A: Assumptions about People

1. What is your personal theory of the basic nature of people?
2. How is this theory reflected in how you actually manage people?
3. Are there any possible downsides or blind spots of your theory?
4. What can you do to deal with these downsides?

## Part B: Meeting Employee Needs in the Workplace

Identify three specific actions that you will take to help your employees meet their motivational needs for achievement, affiliation, and power in the workplace.

CREATING ENGAGEMENT

## Part C: Start, Stop, and Continue

1. What are five specific actions you will START doing today to be a source of motivation for those around you?
2. What are five specific actions you will STOP doing today so that you are not a source of demotivation for others?
3. What are five specific actions that you have been doing and that are already a source of motivation for others that you will CONTINUE to do?

## Part D: Enhancing your Level of Engagement

Identify three specific actions that YOU will take to boost your sense of motivation and engagement at work.

CREATING ENGAGEMENT

# About the Managerial Competencies Series

# What's in the series?

This series is built around four managerial competency clusters: personal, people, purpose, and process.

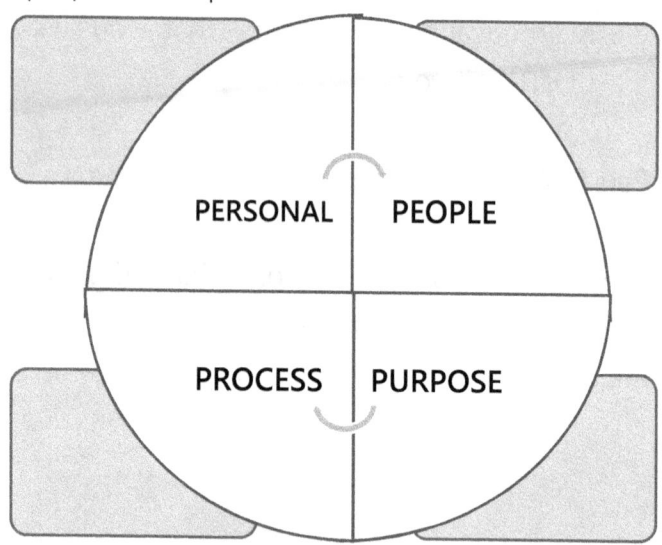

CREATING ENGAGEMENT

Each cluster is made up of several competencies possessed by awesome managers. The series addresses a total of 15 competencies, each of which is the topic of a book of around 100 pages. Let's look at each cluster one at a time.

**Personal Competencies**

The starting point of the series is developing personal skills, given that effective self-management is essential for managing people, programs, and processes. It goes without saying that to manage others, you first must be able to manage yourself. People who are familiar with their personal strengths and challenges and who engage in effective self-management tend to work well with others.

# CREATING ENGAGEMENT

Here are the competencies included in the Personal Competencies cluster:

1. **Living the Core Values**, which involves demonstrating honesty, truthfulness, trustworthiness, reliability, fairness, and ethicality in all your decisions and interactions.
2. **Developing Personal Mastery** through personal responsibility, emotional resilience, constructive attitudes, self-confidence, adaptability, conscientiousness, and competence.
3. **Organizing Yourself** by focusing on your

priorities and making effective use of time.
4. **Building Stress Resilience**, which deals with managing life's stresses by developing personal hardiness.

## People Competencies

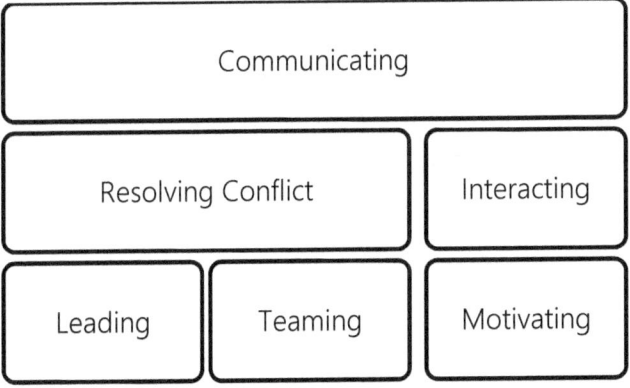

This cluster helps you examine and build your skills in working with and managing others. Although it's important for managers to be *technically* competent in order to gain credibility, interpersonal skills make the difference between awesome and not-so-awesome managers.

## CREATING ENGAGEMENT

The competencies included in the People Competencies cluster are:

5. **Communicating in Writing and through Presentations**, which focuses on communicating ideas effectively, whether verbally or in writing.
6. **Creating Employee Engagement**, creating motivating working conditions so that staff contribute their best to the organization.
7. **Building Relationships**, which considers how to interact with others through effective listening and responding.
8. **Resolving Conflict**, which addresses how to deal with conflict in a productive manner.
9. **Leading Your Team**, which means leading in a manner that is appropriate for the needs of the situation and your team.
10. **Cultivating Team Spirit** by building a cohesive, high-performing team.

CREATING ENGAGEMENT

## Purpose and Process Competencies

This final cluster combines two sets of competencies. Purpose competencies offer you a "big picture" perspective of your organization and your own role in the organization. Process competencies help you translate this "big picture" (the *whats*) into everyday practice (the *hows*). In other words, they allow you to consider how work should be done as a means of accomplishing the goals of your organization and your work unit.

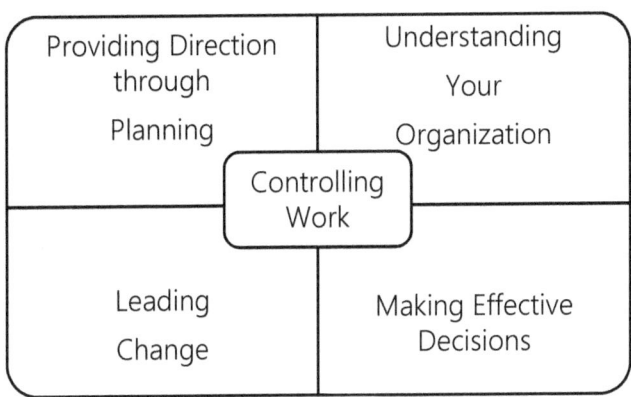

# CREATING ENGAGEMENT

Purpose and Process competencies include:

11. **Making Effective Decisions**, whether individually or in a team setting.
12. **Controlling Work Performance** by establishing control mechanisms to ensure results.
13. **Providing Direction through Planning**, which discusses the management process and offers tips for setting organizational direction and developing operational plans that fit this direction.
14. **Understanding Your Organization**, in other words, understanding the principles of organizing work and creating the right structure for your work unit.
15. **Leading Change** so that your organization and team thrive.

CREATING ENGAGEMENT

# How is each book organized?

Each book is organized according to a five-step learning process. This process is designed to help you learn in an active and reflective manner.

In each book, after a brief introduction, we jump right into the "**reality check**." This series of self-coaching questions is meant to help you reflect on and develop insight into your own strengths and weaknesses in relation to a particular competence and, hopefully,

# CREATING ENGAGEMENT

motivate you to work on building your competencies.

The reality check consists of the kinds of questions that management coaches might ask you, but that you can simply ask yourself. Just be sure to give yourself a chance to answer them!

Management coaches help managers view and understand situations from a variety of perspectives. But, if the art of coaching is asking challenging questions (as management coach Chantal Binet says), why not ask yourself these questions?

Second, to accompany you on your learning journey, you're offered a curated collection of **inspirational quotes**. There's lots of wisdom available from people from all walks of life. The quotes that grab us and speak to us do so because they have touched a nerve in us. They resonate with us, perhaps because they offer a message that we need to hear to continue developing or because they challenge us to become better people.

CREATING ENGAGEMENT

Third, we offer you tons of **tips and tricks** of awesome managers. These practical tips cover a gamut of perspectives and actions that you can take to improve your competencies. Ideally, they will encourage you to consider the variety of possibilities and alternatives that are available to you. It's up to you to decide which are the most useful to you. As you read this section, be sure to note or highlight the tips that stand out for you.

Next, we present a series of **dilemmas** or situations for you to resolve. This section will help you see how you might apply the tips and tricks from the previous section. We ask you to read the situation and then identify what you would do in these situations. You might choose one of the alternatives that is offered, or you might come up with your own creative solution. Ultimately, there are many factors and perspectives that might influence what is the "best" choice.

Finally, we nudge you to develop an **action plan** that you will *actually* implement.

## CREATING ENGAGEMENT

Developing and implementing an action plan is an especially important step because it helps you draw value from your efforts in working through this series. After all, you're reading this book because you're hoping to become an awesome manager, right? This means developing a realistic plan that describes the actions that you intend to take to become an awesome manager, implementing your plan, reflecting on how well it worked, and then continuously making any adjustments that are needed. So, the cycle starts again!

CREATING ENGAGEMENT

# How can you get the most out of the series?

You can read one or two books per month for an entire year, creating and implementing action plans for each book. Ultimately, this will help you develop a better understanding of yourself as a manager, your expectations, your strengths, and your areas for improvement.

As a way of refreshing your competencies, you can even re-read the books and re-visit your action plans in the future. Depending on what's happening in your life (new job, new team, new challenges), every time you read these books, you may develop new insights that help you deal with a situation.

## CREATING ENGAGEMENT

The knowledge of the world is only to be acquired in the world, and not in a closet.
*Lord Chesterfield*

What we have to learn to do,
we learn by doing.
*Aristotle*

Life is a succession of lessons which must be lived to be understood.
*Ralph Waldo Emerson*

What do this British statesman from the 1600s, Greek philosopher from 384 B.C., and American poet from the 1800s have in common? They all agree that learning comes from trying new things, not from simply sitting back and reading a book.

**Don't just read the books; *do* them!** Just reading the books won't transform you into an awesome manager. If you just read the books, you might get to know a lot about what it means to be an awesome manager without

## CREATING ENGAGEMENT

changing what you do in the workplace. How useful is that? Just like learning to ride a bike, it's impossible to develop your skills by simply reading or even thinking about what you have read. Besides, as *The Matrix* reminds us, "There's a difference between knowing the path and walking it."

**In order to truly learn from our experiences, we need to do a complete loop of the learning cycle**: we need to reflect on our experiences, figure out what lessons we learned, consider ways to apply these lessons, and then apply them. You may know people who seem to repeat the same mistakes over and over again or people who continually approach situations in a manner that doesn't work for them. It's probably because they go through life without taking the time to reflect, consider what they've learned, and develop an action plan in order to change their experiences. They're stuck somewhere on the learning cycle. David Kolb, the creator of this learning cycle, says that we all have a favorite

# CREATING ENGAGEMENT

place on the cycle where we tend to get stuck.

Some people simply enjoy reading the books and reflecting on how they may relate to their lives, hopefully finding an opportunity to make use of their learning at some point in the future. However, without specific goals and action plans, they're not extracting as much value as they could from their investment of time and money.

Although this is partly due to differences in learning styles, it's also due to a reluctance to try something new and different. This may be caused by a fear of stepping out of one's comfort zone: what is familiar is comfortable. It may also be caused by a desire to accumulate a truckload of knowledge or have the perfect circumstances, such as the ideal boss or set of employees, before acting. Some of us think and think and continue to think without taking action. That used to be my personal downfall until I realized that knowing lots about a topic isn't the same as learning or making a difference in real life!

CREATING ENGAGEMENT

At the other extreme, some of us take action without first reflecting on our experiences and what we learned from them. Some people prefer to go ahead and try things out right away. They're more action-oriented than their reflective counterparts. These folks typically find it especially challenging to slow down, consciously reflect on what they're reading, and develop a well thought out action plan before acting. In the same way, if you just read the books and do nothing else, the learning process will get stuck right off the bat.

**Reflecting and taking action is the best solution.** It's not enough to *know* how to do something. Although it's helpful and important to take the time to reflect and develop insights, at some point, you need to *do* the work yourself. Otherwise, as management expert Peter Block has said, "Waiting becomes an excuse for not acting."

Here are **five other important things** to do to maximize your learning. First, **keep a learning journal**. Record your thoughts as you

# CREATING ENGAGEMENT

read the books, answer the self-coaching questions, and develop your action plans. It will help you clarify your thinking, see patterns in what you have been experiencing and writing, and serve as a record of commitments you have made to yourself through your action plans. You'll be able to look back at what you've written and be impressed with all that you've learned! You could use a notebook or create an electronic document. Some people even email journal entries to themselves as a way of recording the day and time of their entries.

Second, **pull together a feedback team** who can help you get the most from this series. Your feedback team could be a group of four or five people that you have confidence in, such as coworkers, your manager, friends, and family members. Don't be shy about asking people for their support in helping you become a better manager; they are more willing to help you than you might think! These discussions will offer you different perspectives

## CREATING ENGAGEMENT

and exponentially increase how much you learn from the series. Besides, awesome managers surround themselves with people they trust who are willing to give them honest feedback that will help them grow as individuals.

In supporting you, others can play one or more of the following roles:

→ The Head: These people can help you analyze a question or problem objectively. They can sketch out options, compare data, or simply provide you with accurate information.

→ The Heart: These people can help you express your emotions and understand them better. They listen, cheer you up, don't make judgments, and give you a sense of security.

→ The Legs/Arms: These people help you do things. They go places with you; they make you get moving when you don't feel like it. These people energize you.

# CREATING ENGAGEMENT

**How can your manager help?** Can your manager provide feedback, advice and tips, and time to complete the series? What will you do to get your manager's help? For example, could you meet with your manager once every two weeks to discuss your progress and talk about how to manage effectively?

**How can your peers help?** Can your peers provide feedback, tips about managing, or coaching when needed? What will you do to get their help? Could you schedule a coffee break with them once every two weeks to discuss what you're learning and to share tips? Can you work through the series together?

**How can your employees help?** Can your employees provide feedback regarding your strengths and opportunities for improvement or work with you to develop a plan for making your unit function more effectively? What will you do to get their help? Could you meet with them once every two weeks to discuss what you're learning and how your team can implement elements of your

CREATING ENGAGEMENT

action plan?

**How can your friends help?** Could they provide feedback, tips about managing, and encouragement for you to try new things? What will you do to get their help? Could you organize a dinner with them once every two weeks to discuss what you're learning and how to implement your action plan?

Third, **develop and implement a SMARTER action plan.** You know you've really learned something when your behavior changes (for the better, of course). Insights and tips that are meaningful to you will change your perspective *and* your behaviors. That's why each book ends by inviting you to develop an action plan. Your plan should be **Specific, Measurable, Attainable, Realistic, Timely, Exciting, and Rewarded.** Think about things that you need to start doing, stop doing, or continue doing.

# CREATING ENGAGEMENT

Here's an example: "By the end of next week, I will write two letters – one to my former manager and one to my best friend – expressing my gratitude for their coaching and willingness to challenge me to become a better person. I will send these letters by email no later than Friday afternoon." Write your action plan in your journal. Revisit it to check your progress, and revise your plan as needed. Remember to ask for help from others, evaluate your progress, and reward yourself for your progress toward becoming an awesome manager.

Fourth, **identify obstacles or barriers that might get in your way of making the most of the series** and implementing your action plans; for example, lack of time or energy, poor personal habits, others' expectations, etc. List these in the column labelled "Obstacles" on the following page. Now, think about specific actions that you can take to address them and place these in the "Neutralizers" column; for example, meet with your manager, plan small

## CREATING ENGAGEMENT

wins or ways to celebrate your progress, etc.

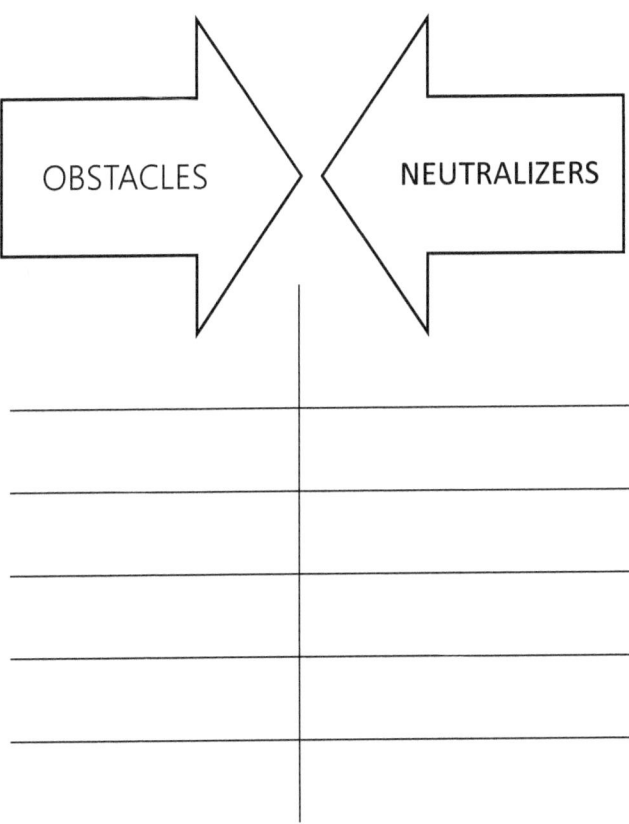

## CREATING ENGAGEMENT

**Finally, do what you need to do to motivate yourself.** Don't wait to be motivated to get started. Instead, get started, and motivation will come knocking at your door!

Also, try to be comfortable with discomfort. As you change how you manage, you may meet with some resistance from those around you. You exist in a system of relationships. Because systems are geared toward equilibrium (stability), if you change one thing in the system, the equilibrium is shot, and the system is upset. There may be pressure from others and from your own sense of comfort for you to do what you've always done regardless of whether or not it works.

It may be tempting to give up when things feel unnatural, but rest assured that this is part of the learning process. It's normal that trying out new ways of doing things makes you feel a bit uncomfortable in one way or another. Sometimes, we come across awesome folks who do their work without hesitation and seemingly without effort. It's easy to forget that

## CREATING ENGAGEMENT

they've gone through the highs and lows of the learning process. For example, think of Cirque du Soleil acrobats who seem to perform stunts with ease and pinpoint accuracy. It took them lots of practice, repetition, and even occasional failures to get to that skill level. Experts make things look easy.

Are you ready to begin your awesome journey? Earl Nightingale once said, "All you need is the plan, the road map, and the courage to press on to your destination." I hope that this series serves as your guide and road map on your journey toward awesomeness.

# CREATING ENGAGEMENT

# REFERENCES

Adler, N.J. (1997). *International dimensions of organizational behavior* (3$^{rd}$ Ed.) Cincinatti, OH: South-Western College Publishing.

Baumeister, R. F. & Leary, M. (1995). The need to belong: Desire for interpersonal attachments as a fundamental human motivation. *Psychological Bulletin*, 117(3), 497-529.

Hackman, J.R. "Work Design," in J.R. Hackman & J.L. Suttle, eds. *Improving Life at Work*. Glenview, IL: Scott Fresman, 1977), p. 129.

Kanfer, R. (1990). Motivation theory and Industrial/Organizational psychology. In M.D. Dunnette and L. Hough (Eds.), *Handbook of industrial and organizational psychology, Vol. 1.* Palo Alto, CA: Consulting Psychologists Press.

Kerr, S. (1995). On the folly of rewarding A, while hoping for B, *Academy of Management Executive,* 9, 7-14.

Manzoni, J.F., & Barsoux, J. (1998). The set-up-to-fail-syndrome. *Harvard Business Review*, 76, 101-113.

Structured Experiences Kit, (1985). University Associates, San Diego.

# CREATING ENGAGEMENT

CREATING ENGAGEMENT

# Playbooks in the Managerial Competencies Series

1. Living the Core Values
2. Developing Personal Mastery
3. Organizing Yourself
4. Building Stress Resilience
5. Communicating in Writing and Through Presentations
6. Creating Employee Engagement
7. Building Relationships
8. Resolving Conflict
9. Leading Your Team
10. Cultivating Team Spirit
11. Making Effective Decisions
12. Controlling Work Performance
13. Providing Direction through Planning
14. Understanding Your Organization
15. Leading Change

www.ingramcontent.com/pod-product-compliance
Lightning Source LLC
Chambersburg PA
CBHW070306230526
45470CB00002B/749